The Bitcoin key

Unlock the world of digital currency

Table of contents

Part 1: Introduction

- **Chapter 1: What is Bitcoin?**
  - The History of Bitcoin
  - The main features of Bitcoin
  - Bitcoin compared to traditional currencies
- **Chapter 2: How Bitcoin Works?**
  - The blockchain technology
  - Transactions and mining
  - Bitcoin wallets
- **Chapter 3: The Future of Bitcoin**
  - Possible areas of application
  - Challenges and risks
  - The future of money

Part 2: Bitcoin in practice

- **Chapter 4: Buying and Selling Bitcoin**
  - Bitcoin exchanges
  - Payment methods
  - Security when buying and selling Bitcoin
- **Chapter 5: Keeping Bitcoin Safe**
  - Types of Bitcoin Wallets
  - Bitcoin wallet security practices

- Hardware wallets
- **Chapter 6: Using Bitcoin**
  - Bitcoin payments in online trading
  - Bitcoin acceptance in the real world
  - Bitcoin applications

Part 3: Advanced topics

- **Chapter 7: Bitcoin Mining**
  - How does Bitcoin mining work?
  - Mining hardware and software
  - The Profitability of Bitcoin Mining
- **Chapter 8: Lightning Network**
  - Scaling solutions for Bitcoin
  - The Lightning Network in detail
  - Use of the Lightning Network
- **Chapter 9: Bitcoin and Blockchain Technology**
  - Areas of application of blockchain
  - Decentralized applications (dApps)
  - The future of blockchain technology

Attachment

- Glossary of important terms
- Resources for further information
- List of Bitcoin exchanges and wallets

Please note that this is not investment advice. It is important to do your research and understand the risks involved before investing in Bitcoin or other cryptocurrencies.

Part 1: Introduction

Chapter 1: What is Bitcoin?

- *The History of Bitcoin*

Prehistory:

- **1980s:** David Chaum develops DigiCash, a digital currency with weak anonymity.
- **1998:** Wei Dai releases "b-money", a decentralized digital currency concept.
- **2008:** Nick Szabo releases "Bit Gold", a proposal for a limited supply digital currency.

2009:

- **January:** Satoshi Nakamoto publishes the Bitcoin white paper and the first Bitcoin software.
- **January 3rd:** The first Bitcoin block ("Genesis Block") is mined.
- **October:** The first Bitcoin transaction takes place: Satoshi Nakamoto sends 10 Bitcoins to Hal Finney.

2010:

- **May:** The first Bitcoin exchange , BitcoinMarket , is founded.
- **November:** Laszlo Hanyecz buys two pizzas for 10,000 Bitcoins - the first Bitcoin transaction for goods.

2011:

- **February:** Mt. Gox , the first major Bitcoin exchange, is founded.
- **June:** The first Bitcoin conference takes place in San Francisco.

2012:

- **April:** The Bitcoin Foundation is founded to promote the development of Bitcoin.
- **November:** The first Bitcoin mining pool is founded.

2013:

- **Cyprus Crisis:** Bitcoin is experiencing a surge in demand due to uncertainty in the financial system.
- **October:** The first Bitcoin ETF (Exchange Traded Fund) is launched on the stock exchange.

2014:

- **February:** The Mt. Gox hack: 850,000 Bitcoins are stolen, causing the exchange to collapse.

2015:

- **October:** The first Bitcoin scaling debate begins.

2016:

- **June:** The DAO hack: 3.6 million Ether (approximately $50 million) are stolen.
- **August:** Bitcoin Cash (BCH) splits from Bitcoin.

2017:

- **December:** Bitcoin hits an all-time high of nearly $20,000.

2018:

- **Crypto winter:** The Bitcoin price falls sharply and reaches $3,100 in December.

2019:

- **June:** Facebook announces Libra , a digital currency based on a blockchain.
- **October:** China bans Bitcoin mining.

2020:

- **March:** The COVID-19-related crash: The Bitcoin price briefly falls to $3,800.

- **December:** Bitcoin hits another all-time high of almost $29,000.

2021:

- **February:** Tesla invests $1.5 billion in Bitcoin.
- **April:** Bitcoin hits a new all-time high of $64,800.
- **May:** China bans Bitcoin transactions.
- **November:** El Salvador adopts Bitcoin as legal tender.

2022:

- **January:** Bitcoin price falls below $40,000.
- **February:** Russia considers accepting Bitcoin as payment for oil and gas.
- **May:** TerraUSD (UST) and Luna crash, leading to a crypto crash.
- **June:** Celsius Network and Three Arrows Capital report bankruptcy .

2023:

- **January:** Bitcoin price falls below $30,000.
- **February:** The SEC rejects a Bitcoin ETF.
- **March:** Bitcoin price rises above $40,000 again.

2024:

- **(As of March 2nd):** Bitcoin price is around 42,000 US dollars.
-

- *The main features of Bitcoin*

- **Decentralization:** Bitcoin is decentralized, meaning there is no central authority that controls the network. Instead, it is powered by a network of computers around the world. This makes Bitcoin resistant to manipulation and censorship.
- **Security:** Bitcoin is secured by cryptography, which makes it very safe from counterfeiting and fraud. The blockchain that underlies Bitcoin is an immutable public ledger that records all transactions.
- **Transparency:** All transactions on the Bitcoin blockchain are publicly visible. This allows anyone to review transaction history and ensure that all transactions were executed correctly.
- **Pseudonymity :** Bitcoin users can conduct transactions pseudonymously, meaning they do not have to reveal their identity. This allows them to protect their privacy.
- **Cross-border transactions:** Bitcoin transactions can be carried out quickly and easily worldwide. There are no fees for cross-border transactions.
- **Fungibility:** Bitcoins are fungible, meaning each Bitcoin is equivalent. This makes Bitcoin an ideal medium of exchange.
- **Limited quantity:** There will only be a limited number of Bitcoins, namely 21 million. This makes Bitcoin a deflationary asset, meaning its value should increase over time.

- **Openness:** Bitcoin is an open source project, meaning anyone can participate in the network and develop it further.
- **Innovation:** Bitcoin is an innovative technology with the potential to revolutionize finance.
- **Risk:** Bitcoin is a volatile investment vehicle. The value of Bitcoin can fluctuate greatly.
- **Regulation:** Bitcoin is not yet regulated in many countries. This can lead to legal uncertainty.
- **Scalability:** The Bitcoin blockchain is currently not very scalable. This can lead to bottlenecks in transaction processing.
- **Sustainability:** The Bitcoin mining process uses a lot of energy. This can lead to environmental problems.
- **In summary, Bitcoin is a unique technology with many advantages. However, it is important to also be aware of the risks before investing in Bitcoin.**
- *Bitcoin compared to traditional currencies*

Decentralization:

- Bitcoin is decentralized, meaning there is no central authority that has control over the currency.
- Traditional currencies are controlled by central banks, which can influence the money supply and the value of the currency.

Transparency:

- All Bitcoin transactions are transparent and visible on the blockchain.
- Transactions involving traditional currencies can be opaque, especially when conducted through cash or offshore accounts.

Anonymity:

- Bitcoin transactions are pseudonymous, meaning the identities of the senders and recipients are not directly visible.
- Traditional currencies are usually linked to the user's identity.

Volatility:

- The Bitcoin price is highly fluctuating and volatile.
- Traditional currencies tend to be more stable because they are regulated by central banks.

Acceptance:

- Bitcoin is not yet widely accepted as a means of payment.
- Conventional currencies are established as means of payment worldwide.

Scalability:

- The Bitcoin network currently has limited scalability, meaning it can only process a limited number of transactions per second.
- Traditional currency systems tend to be more scalable.

Future:

- The future of Bitcoin and cryptocurrencies is uncertain.
- Traditional currencies are likely to continue to play the dominant role in the global financial system.

In summary, Bitcoin and traditional currencies have both advantages and disadvantages. Bitcoin offers more decentralization, transparency and anonymity, but is more volatile and less accepted. Traditional currencies are more stable and established, but less transparent and anonymous.

Which currency is more suitable depends on the individual needs and preferences of the user.

Additional Information:

- Bitcoin Wiki: https://en.bitcoin.it/wiki/Main_Page
- European Central Bank: https://www.ecb.europa.eu/
- International Monetary Fund: https://www.imf.org/

Please note that this is not investment advice. It is important to do your research and understand the risks involved before investing in Bitcoin or other cryptocurrencies.

- **Chapter 2: How Bitcoin Works?**

   - *The blockchain technology*

Blockchain technology, also known as distributed ledger technology, is an innovative method to store and manage data securely and transparently. You can think of the blockchain as a digital ledger that is shared by multiple participants.

Here are some key aspects of blockchain:

- **Decentralization:** Instead of a central authority controlling the data, the blockchain is stored distributed across a network of computers. This makes it tamper-proof as any attempt to change data would be noticed on all systems on the network.
- **Transparency:** All participants in the network have access to the same copy of the blockchain. This creates trust and enables transactions to be tracked.
- **Security:** Cryptographic procedures ensure that data in the blockchain cannot be forged.

Blockchain technology offers a wide range of possible uses, for example:

- **Finance:** Cryptocurrencies like Bitcoin are based on the blockchain.
- **Supply chains:** Blockchain can track the origin of goods and prevent counterfeiting.
- **Voting:** Blockchain technology could enable secure and transparent elections.

Although blockchain technology has great potential, many applications are still in the development phase. There are also challenges such as the scalability and energy consumption of certain blockchain systems

- *Transactions and mining*

Transactions:

- Bitcoin transactions are digital transfers of Bitcoins from one wallet to another.
- They are secured by digital signatures and recorded on the blockchain.
- Every transaction must be verified by a miner before being added to the blockchain.
- Transaction fees vary depending on network load and priority.

Mining:

- Mining is the process of verifying transactions and creating new blocks on the blockchain.
- Miners use powerful computers to solve complex mathematical problems.
- The first miner to solve a problem is rewarded with Bitcoins.
- Mining is an important part of the Bitcoin network as it ensures the security and decentralization of the system.

More details:

- **Transaction details:**
    - sender and recipient
    - Transaction amount
    - fees
    - Transaction ID
- **Mining process:**
    - Miners collect transactions in a block.
    - You solve a math problem to validate the block.
    - The new block is appended to the blockchain.
    - Miners receive rewards in the form of Bitcoins.
- **Mining hardware:**
    - ASIC miners: powerful, specialized devices
    - GPUs: graphics cards
    - CPUs: central processors
- **Criticism of mining:**
    - high energy consumption

- Centralization of the mining pool

Resources:

- Bitcoin Wiki: Transactions : https://en.bitcoin.it/wiki/Transaction
- Bitcoin Wiki: Mining: https://en.bitcoin.it/wiki/Mining
- Bitpanda Academy: Bitcoin Mining: [invalid URL removed]
- BTC-ECHO: Bitcoin mining: https://www.btc-echo.de/academy/bibliothek/was-ist-bitcoin-mining/

- *Bitcoin wallets*

Bitcoin wallets, also known as digital wallets, are used to securely store, send and receive Bitcoin. However, similar to a traditional wallet where you store cash, a Bitcoin wallet does not store physical coins, but rather **private keys that** allow access to your Bitcoin .

Here are some important points about Bitcoin wallets:

- **They don't store Bitcoins themselves:** Bitcoin exists on a decentralized network called a blockchain. The wallet simply stores the keys that you can use to prove that certain Bitcoins belong to you.

- **Public and private keys:** Every wallet has two important keys:
  - **Public key:** This is used to receive Bitcoins. It is comparable to an IBAN and can be freely passed on as it is needed to send Bitcoins.
  - **Private key:** This is secret and should never be shared. It allows you to access your Bitcoins and sign transactions.
- **Different Types of Bitcoin Wallets:** There are different types of Bitcoin wallets that differ in terms of security, ease of use, and features. Common types include:
  - **Hot Wallets:** These are connected to the internet and provide an easy way to send and receive Bitcoins. However, they are also more susceptible to hacks.
  - **Cold wallets:** These are not connected to the internet and therefore offer greater security. However, they are less practical for everyday use.

It is important that you do your research before choosing a Bitcoin wallet and choose the one that best suits your security and functionality needs.

Chapter 3: The Future of Bitcoin

- *Possible areas of application*

Bitcoin is the first and best-known cryptocurrency and has the potential to revolutionize various areas of application. Here are some of the most important ones:

1. Means of payment: Bitcoin can be used as a digital means of payment for goods and services. It offers several advantages over traditional payment methods such as: E.g.:

- **Lower fees:** Transactions on the Bitcoin blockchain are usually significantly cheaper than transactions with credit cards or bank transfers.
- **Faster Transactions:** Bitcoin transactions are typically processed within a few minutes, while traditional transactions can take several days.
- **Cross-border payments:** Bitcoin transactions are not limited by national borders and can therefore be carried out quickly and easily worldwide.

2. Store of Value: Bitcoin can be used as a store of value, similar to gold or stocks. The quantity of Bitcoin is limited, which can help maintain its value over time.

3. Investment: Bitcoin can be used as an investment object. The Bitcoin price is volatile, which means that there can be both large profits and losses.

4. Decentralized Financial Services (DeFi): Bitcoin can be used in DeFi applications, e.g. B. to lend or borrow loans, earn interest or trade on decentralized exchanges.

5. Use cases beyond finance: Bitcoin can also be used in other application areas, e.g. E.g.:

- **Identity Management:** Bitcoin can be used to create and manage digital identities.
- **Supply Chain Management:** Bitcoin can be used to track and secure the supply chain of goods.
- **Voting Systems:** Bitcoin can be used to create secure and transparent voting systems.

It should be noted that Bitcoin is still a relatively young technology and the areas of application are constantly evolving.

For more information about Bitcoin, visit the following websites:

- https://bitcoin.org/
- BitcoinWiki : https://en.bitcoin.it/wiki/Main_Page
- CoinMarketCap : https://coinmarketcap.com/

- Challenges and risks

- Bitcoin has become one of the most well-known and valuable cryptocurrencies since its launch in 2009. However, the following challenges and risks should be considered before investing in Bitcoin:
- **Volatility:** The Bitcoin price is extremely volatile, meaning that it is subject to strong and sudden fluctuations. This can lead to high profits but also significant losses.
- **Technical risks:** Bitcoin technology is complex and there is a risk of hacker attacks, software errors or other technical problems.
- **Regulation:** The legal situation of Bitcoin is still unclear in many countries. Regulatory measures could affect the value and usage of Bitcoin.
- **Scalability:** The Bitcoin network is currently unable to handle large transaction volumes. This can lead to long waiting times and high transaction fees.
- **Sustainability:** Bitcoin mining, the process of creating new Bitcoins, uses large amounts of energy. This can lead to environmental problems.
- **Risk of Loss:** Bitcoin wallets may be lost or stolen. Since there is no central authority that can help with losses, the risk of a total loss is high.
- **Criminal Use:** Bitcoin has been used in the past for illegal activities such as money laundering and drug trafficking. This could lead to a negative image and tightening of regulation.
- **Investor protection:** There is no investor protection for Bitcoin investments. Investors are therefore

exposed to the risk of fraud and market manipulation.
- **Lack of intrinsic value :** Unlike stocks or bonds, which represent a claim to a certain value or future cash flows, Bitcoin has no intrinsic value. The value of Bitcoin is based solely on supply and demand.
- **High barriers to entry:** Operating Bitcoin wallets and using Bitcoin exchanges can be complicated and confusing for beginners.
- **Spread:** Bitcoin is not yet widely used and is not accepted by many companies and merchants.
- **Future uncertain:** The future of Bitcoin is uncertain. It is possible that Bitcoin will catch on and become an important part of the global financial system. But it is also possible that Bitcoin will become less important or even disappear completely.
- **Conclusion:** Bitcoin is a risky investment. Investors should be aware of the above challenges and risks before investing in Bitcoin.

- *The future of money*

The future of money is a topic that has been debated for a long time. There are many different opinions about how money will develop in the future. Some believe that cash will be completely replaced by digital currencies, while others believe that cash will always play an important role.

There are several trends that could influence the future of money. This includes:

- **The increasing digitalization of the global economy:** More and more people are using digital payment methods such as credit cards, debit cards and online payment systems.
- **The development of new technologies:** New technologies such as blockchain and cryptocurrencies could have the potential to fundamentally change the monetary system.
- **The growing importance of central banks:** Central banks are playing an increasingly important role in regulating the monetary system.

It is difficult to say with certainty how money will develop in the future. However, it is likely that the monetary system will undergo significant changes in the coming years and decades.

Possible scenarios for the future of money:

- **Cashless Payment System:** In a cashless payment system, all transactions would be processed electronically. This would increase the efficiency and security of the payment system, but could also reduce people's privacy and control over their money.
- **Cryptocurrency Dominance:** Cryptocurrencies are digital currencies based on blockchain technology. They are decentralized and not tied to a central bank or government. Cryptocurrencies could play a more important role in the future, but there are also challenges such as high volatility and lack of regulation.
- **Central Bank Digital Currencies (CBDCs):** CBDCs are digital currencies issued by central banks. They could combine the advantages of cash

and digital currencies, but they could also increase central banks' control over the money supply.

The future of money is uncertain, but it is an issue that is important to everyone. It is important to inform yourself about the possible developments and prepare for the changes that could come.

Part 2: Bitcoin in practice

Chapter 4: Buying and Selling Bitcoin

- *Bitcoin exchanges*

There are a variety of Bitcoin exchanges that vary in terms of fees, trading volume, supported cryptocurrencies, and features. Here are some of the most popular Bitcoin exchanges:

Centralized Exchanges:

- **Octopuses:** https://www.nhl.com/kraken/ - One of the oldest and most established Bitcoin exchanges

with high liquidity and a wide range of cryptocurrencies.
- **Binance :** https://www.binance.com/en - The largest cryptocurrency exchange in the world with huge trading volume and a variety of cryptocurrencies and trading pairs.
- **Coinbase:** https://www.coinbase.com/ - A user-friendly exchange ideal for beginners that offers a limited number of cryptocurrencies.
- **Bitpanda :** https://www.bitpanda.com/en - A European exchange with an intuitive interface and a focus on the Euro area.
- **eToro:** https://www.etoro.com/ - A social trading platform that also offers cryptocurrency trading.

Decentralized exchanges:

- **Uniswap :** https://uniswap.org/ - A decentralized exchange that allows cryptocurrency trading without intermediaries.
- **PancakeSwap :** https://pancakeswap.finance/ - A decentralized exchange on the Binance Smart Chain that specializes in exchanging BEP-20 tokens.
- **SushiSwap :** https://www.sushi.com/ - A decentralized exchange that uses forks of Uniswap code and offers additional features such as staking and yield farming.

More Bitcoin exchanges:

- **Bitcoin.de:** https://www.bitcoin.de/en - A German exchange with a focus on Bitcoin and Euro.

- **BSDEX:** https://www.bsdex.de/en/ - A German exchange with high security standards and a focus on Bitcoin.
- **Nuri:** https://www.instagram.com/theofficialnuri/ - A German exchange with an intuitive interface and the ability to buy Bitcoin via bank transfer.

Important NOTE:

Before choosing a Bitcoin exchange, you should find out about the following points:

- **Fees:** Fees for trading Bitcoin can vary greatly. Compare the fees of different exchanges before choosing one.
- **Trading volume:** The trading volume of an exchange is an indicator of the liquidity of the market. Make sure that the exchange has sufficient trading volume for the cryptocurrencies you want.
- **Security:** The security of your Bitcoin is of utmost importance. Choose an exchange with a good reputation and high security standards.
- **Supported Cryptocurrencies:** Not all exchanges support all cryptocurrencies. Make sure the exchange offers the cryptocurrencies you want.
- **Features:** Some exchanges offer additional features such as staking , margin trading, and lending. These features may be of interest to experienced traders.

- *Payment methods*

There are various payment methods to buy or sell Bitcoin, which may differ depending on the platform and region. Here are some common options:

When buying Bitcoin:

- **SEPA transfer:** This is the most common method in Germany. You simply transfer money from your bank account to the platform you want to buy Bitcoin from.
- **Credit or debit card:** Some platforms, such as hardware wallet providers, allow you to purchase Bitcoin using a credit or debit card. However, there are often fees for this.
- **Express trading:** On some platforms, such as Bitcoin.de, you can choose the express trading option. The purchase price is immediately deducted from your bank account at the platform's partner bank and you receive the Bitcoins in return.
- **Peer-to-peer trading (P2P):** With this method, you trade directly with other people without any platform in between. The payment methods can be very diverse, from cash to transfers.

When selling Bitcoin:

- **Transfer:** As a rule, when selling Bitcoin on a platform, you will receive bank details to which the buyer must transfer the money.
- **Express trading:** On some platforms, such as Bitcoin.de, you can also sell your Bitcoins via express trading. The purchase price will be automatically transferred to your bank account at the platform's partner bank.

Important to note:

- Payment method availability may vary by platform and region. Therefore, always find out in advance what options are available on your chosen platform.
- There are usually fees when purchasing Bitcoin with a credit or debit card.
- Be particularly careful when trading peer-to-peer as the risk of fraud is higher.

- *Security when buying and selling Bitcoin*

Buying and selling Bitcoin involves some risks that are important to be aware of. Here are some tips on how to increase security when trading Bitcoin:

Choosing the right platform:

- Choose a reputable and established trading platform with high security standards.
- Find out about the platform's fees and trading conditions.
- Pay attention to reviews and experiences from other users.

Wallet security:

- Use a secure wallet to store your Bitcoins.
- Hardware wallets that are stored offline are recommended.
- Secure your wallet with a strong password and 2-factor authentication.

Transactions:

- Be wary of phishing attempts and fake websites.
- Please check the recipient address carefully before making a transaction.
- Use a strong password for your trading account.

General safety tips:

- Find out about the current security risks associated with Bitcoin.
- Keep your software and operating systems up to date.
- Use a reliable antivirus program.
- Be wary of offers that sound too good to be true.

Additional Information:

- Bitcoin Security: [invalid URL removed]
- Bitcoin wallets: [invalid URL removed]
- Common Bitcoin Security Questions: [invalid URL removed]

A notice:

The tips above are general advice and do not guarantee the security of your Bitcoins. It is important that you educate yourself about the risks and take appropriate safety measures.

Chapter 5: Keeping Bitcoin Safe

- *Types of Bitcoin Wallets*

There are different types of Bitcoin wallets, each with their own advantages and disadvantages. The most important categories are:

Online wallets:

- Convenient and easy to use as they are accessible via a web browser.
- Less secure than other types of wallets as the private keys are stored on the provider's servers.
- Suitable for smaller amounts that are used frequently.

Mobile wallets:

- Similar to online wallets, but usable on smartphones and tablets.
- Convenient for payments on the go.
- Similar level of security to online wallets.

Desktop wallets:

- Software that is installed on your computer.
- Offers more control over private keys than online wallets.
- May be more vulnerable to malware if the computer is not adequately protected.

Hardware wallets:

- Physical devices that store your private keys offline.
- Offer the highest level of security because the private keys are never connected to the internet.
- Can be a little more complicated to set up for beginners.

Paper wallets:

- Physical documents that have your public and private keys printed on them.
- Extremely secure as they are completely offline.

- Can easily be lost or damaged.

Choosing the right wallet depends on your individual needs and risk tolerance. If you want to store large amounts of Bitcoins, you should consider a hardware wallet. For smaller amounts that you use frequently, a mobile or online wallet may be sufficient.

It is important to note that with all types of wallets, you must always keep your private keys safe. If you lose your private keys, you will also lose access to your Bitcoins.

- Bitcoin wallet security practices

Bitcoin wallets are essential for safely handling your digital assets. However, they also pose security risks if not properly protected. Here are some important security practices to keep in mind for your Bitcoin wallet:

Strong passwords and 2-factor authentication (2FA):

- Always use **long and complex passwords** that contain uppercase and lowercase letters, numbers and special characters. Avoid using personal information or easy-to-guess words.
- Enable **2-factor authentication (2FA)** for your wallet. This adds an additional layer of security by requiring a second verification code on transactions.

Choice of wallet type:

- Choose a **reputed and trustworthy wallet application**. Research and compare different providers before choosing an option.
- **Avoid storing Bitcoins on online wallets**, except for small amounts that you use regularly. Online wallets are more vulnerable to attacks. Consider using **hardware wallets** for larger amounts as these are stored offline and provide an additional layer of security.

Be careful when sharing information:

- **Never** share your private keys or seed phrases with anyone, including employees of supposed support services. Bitcoin transactions are irreversible, and access to this information allows others to steal your Bitcoins.
- Be **wary of links and attachments** in emails or messages that claim to come from legitimate services such as exchanges or wallet providers. These could be phishing attempts aimed at stealing your credentials.

Regular backups:

- Make **regular backups** of your wallet data, especially for hardware wallets. Keep these backups in a safe place, separate from your computer or smartphone.

Updates and virus protection:

- keep your **wallet software and operating system up to date** to benefit from the latest security updates.
- Use **up-to-date and reliable antivirus software** on your device to protect yourself from malware that could attack your wallet.

Additional tips:

- Be **wary of unrealistic profit promises** associated with Bitcoin investing.
- **Learn as much as you can** about Bitcoin and the risks involved before investing.

With these security practices, you can significantly reduce the risk of theft or loss of your Bitcoins. Remember that constant caution and the use of reliable security measures are crucial to protecting your digital assets.

- *Hardware wallets*

Hardware wallets are considered the safest method to store Bitcoins. They essentially act as small, secure computers that store your private keys offline. Unlike software wallets stored on computers or smartphones, hardware wallets cannot be infected by hackers, even if the device they are connected to is compromised.

Here are some key points about hardware wallets for Bitcoin:

- **High security:** Your private keys are never stored online, protecting them from malware and hacker attacks.
- **Transaction Signing:** You can securely sign transactions on the hardware wallet before they are sent to the network.
- **Ease of use:** Modern hardware wallets are easy to use and often have intuitive user interfaces.
- **Well-known manufacturers:** Popular brands for hardware wallets include Ledger and Trezor .

It is important to purchase your hardware wallet from a reputable retailer and carefully follow the manufacturer's safety precautions. This particularly includes safely storing your recovery phrase, which is needed to recover your Bitcoin balance in the event of loss or damage to the hardware wallet.

Chapter 6: Using Bitcoin

- *Bitcoin payments in online trading*

Advantages:

- **Fast and secure:** Bitcoin transactions are usually processed quickly and are very secure thanks to blockchain technology.
- **Cheap:** The transaction fees for Bitcoin payments are significantly lower than for credit cards or other payment methods.
- **Global:** Bitcoin is a global currency that can be used worldwide. This is particularly beneficial for merchants serving international customers.
- **Anonymity:** Bitcoin payments can be made anonymously. This can be beneficial for both buyers and sellers.

Disadvantages:

- **Volatility:** The Bitcoin price fluctuates greatly. This can pose a risk for traders as they have to smooth out price fluctuations.
- **Complexity:** Using Bitcoin can be complicated for some buyers and sellers.

- **Acceptance:** Bitcoin is not yet as widespread as other payment methods.

Acceptance of Bitcoin payments:

More and more online retailers are accepting Bitcoin payments. Some of the best-known providers are:

- **Shopify**
- **Etsy**
- **Overstock**
- **Newegg**
- **Microsoft**

This is how payment with Bitcoin works:

To pay with Bitcoin in online trading you need:

- **A Bitcoin wallet:** This is a digital wallet where you can store your Bitcoins.
- **Bitcoins:** You can buy Bitcoins on a Bitcoin exchange or receive them from other people.

Proceed:

1. In the online store, select the "Bitcoin payment" option.
2. Enter the store's Bitcoin address.
3. Transfer the Bitcoin amount from your wallet to the shop address.
4. The transaction is verified on the blockchain.
5. Once the transaction is confirmed, your order will be shipped.

Conclusion:

Bitcoin payments offer several advantages for both buyers and sellers. Bitcoin acceptance is steadily increasing, and paying with Bitcoin is easy and secure.

Additional Information:

- Bitcoin Wiki: https://en.bitcoin.it/wiki/Main_Page
- Bitcoin FAQ: https://bitcoin.org/faq

- *Bitcoin acceptance in the real world*

The acceptance of Bitcoin as a means of payment in the real world is steadily growing, but there are still some challenges that need to be overcome.

Progress:

- **Numerous companies accept Bitcoin:**
    - Major companies like Tesla, Microsoft and PayPal accept Bitcoin as a payment method.
    - Many small businesses and retailers in various industries, such as restaurants, hotels and online shops, also offer Bitcoin payments.
- **Bitcoin ATMs:**
    - There are over 38,000 Bitcoin ATMs worldwide where you can buy and sell Bitcoins.
    - This makes Bitcoin easier to access for people who are unbanked or don't want to buy cryptocurrencies online.
- **Integration into financial systems:**
    - Crypto exchanges and wallets make it easy to buy, sell and hold Bitcoin.

- Some banks and payment providers offer Bitcoin services, such as Bitcoin custody or the ability to send and receive Bitcoin payments.

Challenges:

- **Volatility:**
  - The value of Bitcoin can fluctuate widely, making its use as a payment method unattractive for some businesses and consumers.
- **Regulation:**
  - Regulation of Bitcoin and cryptocurrencies is inconsistent worldwide, which can make adoption by businesses difficult.
- **Technical hurdles:**
  - Not all people have the technical knowledge or infrastructure to use Bitcoin payments.
- **Understanding and acceptance:**
  - Bitcoin is still a relatively new technology and many people are unaware of the benefits and risks.

Future:

Real-world adoption of Bitcoin is expected to continue to grow over the next few years. The following factors could promote this:

- **Bitcoin Infrastructure Development:**
  - The development of Bitcoin wallets, payment processors and other solutions will make using Bitcoin easier and more convenient.
- **Institutional involvement:**

- ○ If more institutional investors invest in Bitcoin, it could increase adoption by businesses and consumers.
- **Regulatory clarity:**
  - ○ Clearer regulatory frameworks could encourage corporate adoption of Bitcoin.

In summary, real-world adoption of Bitcoin is growing, but there are still some challenges to overcome. The development of Bitcoin infrastructure, participation from institutional investors and clearer regulation could further promote Bitcoin adoption in the next few years.

Additional Information:

- Bitcoin Acceptance Map: https://coinmap.org/

- *Bitcoin applications*

Bitcoin is the best-known cryptocurrency and also the first application of blockchain technology.

Bitcoin as a means of payment:

- **Online Payments:** Bitcoin can be used to purchase goods and services online.
- **Offline payments:** More and more stores are accepting Bitcoin as a payment method.
- **Cross-border payments:** Bitcoin transactions are cross-border and fee-free.

- **Donations:** Bitcoin can be used for donations to NGOs and other organizations.

Bitcoin as an investment:

- **Store of Value:** Bitcoin can serve as a store of value in times of inflation.
- **Asset Class:** Bitcoin can be used as an alternative asset class to stocks and bonds.
- **Speculation:** Bitcoin can be used for speculation due to its volatility.

Other applications of Bitcoin technology:

- **Smart Contracts :** Decentralized applications (dApps) on the Bitcoin blockchain enable the automated execution of contracts.
- **Identity Management:** Bitcoin can be used to securely store identity data.
- **Supply chain management:** Blockchain can be used to track goods in the supply chain.

Limitations of Bitcoin:

- **Volatility:** The Bitcoin price fluctuates greatly.
- **Scalability:** The Bitcoin blockchain is not as scalable as other blockchains.
- **Acceptance:** Bitcoin is not yet as widespread as traditional currencies.

Future of Bitcoin:

The future of Bitcoin is uncertain. It is possible that Bitcoin will become a global currency. But it is also possible that Bitcoin will be replaced by other cryptocurrencies or technologies.

Additional Information:

- Bitcoin Wiki: https://en.bitcoin.it/wiki/Main_Page
- Bitcoin FAQ: https://bitcoin.org/faq
- Bitcoin rate: https://coinmarketcap.com/currencies/bitcoin/

Part 3: Advanced Topics

Chapter 7: Bitcoin Mining

- *How does Bitcoin mining work?*

Basics:

- **Blockchain:** Bitcoin uses a blockchain to store transactions. New transactions are grouped into blocks and appended to the blockchain.
- **Miners:** Miners are computers that create these blocks and secure the blockchain.
- **Mining Hardware:** Miners require specialized hardware to solve complex mathematical problems.
- **Reward:** The first miner to solve a problem receives Bitcoins as a reward.

Process:

1. **Transactions:** Bitcoin transactions are broadcast on the network.
2. **Block formation:** Miners collect transactions and bundle them into blocks.
3. **Hashing :** The block is encrypted using a hashing algorithm.
4. **Mining:** Miners try to find a specific hash value that validates the block.
5. **Validation:** The first miner to find the hash value validates the block and adds it to the blockchain.
6. **Reward:** The miner receives Bitcoins as a reward.

Difficulty level:

- The difficulty of the hash problem is automatically adjusted.
- Goal: Block time of approx. 10 minutes.
- Increasing hashrate -> higher difficulty.

Today:

- **Cloud mining: possibility to** mine without own hardware.
- **Mining pools:** Miners pool their computing power.
- **High energy costs:** Bitcoin mining uses a lot of electricity.

Additional Information:

- Bitcoin mining: what is it & how does mining work? - Bitpanda: https://www.bitpanda.com/academy/de/lektionen/what-is-bitcoin-mining-and-how-works-it
- Bitcoin mining: explanation, energy consumption and co. - WirtschaftsWoche: https://www.wiwo.de/finanzen/boerse/bitcoin-mining-erklaert-wie-funktioniert-bitcoin-mining-und-wie-hoch-ist-der-energy-consumption-really/28866416.html
- How does Bitcoin mining work? Crypto mining explained clearly | ETC Group: https://etc-group.com/de/blog/krypto-handbuch/krypto-mining/

- *Mining hardware and software*

Bitcoin mining requires specialized hardware designed to perform complex mathematical calculations. This hardware will as **ASIC miner** (Application-Specific Integrated Circuit) .

Opens in a new window
a www.amazon.de
ASIC Miner for Bitcoin

ASIC miners are powerful devices specifically designed for Bitcoin mining. They are significantly more efficient than CPUs or GPUs (Graphics Processing Units) previously used for mining.

Bitcoin mining software

In addition to the hardware, you also need special software to mine Bitcoin . The software connects your ASIC miner to the Bitcoin network and allows you to solve the blocks that generate new Bitcoins.

Some popular Bitcoin mining software are:

- **CGMiner :** An open source software compatible with a wide range of ASIC miners .
- **BFGMiner :** Another open source software known for its ease of use.
- **EasyMiner :** An easy-to-use software that is good for beginners.

It is important to note that Bitcoin mining can be profitable, but it is also a highly competitive business. Before you start mining, you should do your research thoroughly and carefully consider the costs and risks involved

- . *The Profitability of Bitcoin Mining*

The profitability of Bitcoin mining depends on several factors that can constantly change:

1. Bitcoin course:

- The most important factor is the Bitcoin price. If the price increases, the profitability of mining also increases . If the price falls, profitability decreases.

- Currently (as of March 3, 2024) the Bitcoin price is around 48,000 USD.

2. Mining Difficulty:

- The difficulty of mining increases with the number of miners. The more miners there are, the harder it becomes to find a block and get the reward.
- The difficulty is readjusted every 2,016 blocks (approximately every two weeks).

3. Electricity costs:

- The cost of electricity is another important factor. The higher the electricity costs, the less profitable mining is.
- The energy consumption of Bitcoin mining devices can be very high.
- It is important to choose a location with cheap electricity costs to increase profitability.

4. Hardware costs:

- The cost of mining hardware is also an important factor.
- There are different types of mining hardware such as: B. ASIC miner and GPU miner.
- ASIC miners are more powerful and efficient than GPU miners, but are also more expensive.

5. Mining pool:

- Many miners join a mining pool to increase their chances of receiving rewards.
- In a mining pool, the blocks are mined together and the reward is divided among the participants.

Profitability calculator:

There are various profitability calculators online that you can use to calculate the profitability of Bitcoin mining .

Example:

- With a current Bitcoin price of $48,000, an electricity cost of $0.10/kWh, and an ASIC miner with a hashrate of 100 TH/s, a miner would earn approximately $10 per day.

Conclusion:

mining profitability can change quickly. It is important to consider all factors before starting mining.

Additional Information:

- Bitcoin Mining Profitability Calculator: https://www.nicehash.com/profitability-calculator
- Bitcoin Mining: Explanation, energy consumption and co.: https://www.wiwo.de/finanzen/boerse/bitcoin-mining-erklaert-wie-funktioniert-bitcoin-mining-und-wie-hoch-ist-der-energieverbrauch-really/28866416.html
- Is Bitcoin Mining Profitable?: https://fastercapital.com/de/content/Ist-Bitcoin-Mining-profitable.html

Chapter 8: Lightning Network

- *Scaling solutions for Bitcoin*

Bitcoin faces a challenge: **scalability** . The network is designed to be secure by limiting the number of transactions per second. However, this leads to slow transaction times and high fees when demand increases.

To address this problem, various **scaling solutions have been** proposed:

- **Lightning Network:** The Lightning Network is a "Layer 2" payment network built on top of the Bitcoin blockchain. It enables fast and low-cost transactions off the main chain by opening payment channels between participants. These channels process transactions off the blockchain and are only recorded on the blockchain if a dispute arises.
- **Increase block size:** Another approach is to increase the block size. This would allow more transactions to be included in each block, increasing transaction speed. However, there are concerns that this could impact the decentralization and security of the network as it would make it more difficult for individual miners to store and validate the entire blockchain.
- **SegWit (Segregated Witness):** SegWit is a soft fork that does not change the block size, but changes the data structure of the blocks. This creates more space for transaction data without

compromising security. SegWit is already implemented and supported by most Bitcoin full nodes.

- **Schnorr Signatures:** Schnorr Signatures are another soft fork that can reduce transaction size. This would in turn allow more transactions into each block. The implementation of Schnorr signatures is still under discussion.

It is important to note that the Bitcoin scaling debate remains controversial. Proponents of the various solutions have different views on which approach is best for Bitcoin. It is likely that a combination of different solutions will be used in the future to improve Bitcoin's scalability.

- *The Lightning Network in detail*

The Lightning Network: Fast payments for Bitcoin

The Lightning Network (LN) is an innovative technology designed to improve Bitcoin's scalability. It is a so-called "second layer solution" that is built on top of the existing Bitcoin blockchain.

Here are some important aspects of the Lightning Network:

Problem: Bitcoin currently has limited transaction speeds because every transaction must be stored on the blockchain. This can result in slow and expensive transactions.

Solution: The Lightning Network allows users to carry out transactions **off** the blockchain. These "off-chain" transactions are significantly faster and cheaper than regular Bitcoin transactions.

Functionality:

- **Channels:** Users open so-called "channels" with each other in which they "hold" Bitcoins. They can then send as many payments back and forth as they want within these channels without putting a strain on the blockchain.
- **Smart Contracts :** The channels use special contracts (smart contracts) that ensure that the Bitcoins held can only be paid out to the rightful recipient.
- **Settlement:** If users in the channel cannot agree, the original sum can be restored on the blockchain.

Advantages:

- **Fast transactions:** Payments on the Lightning Network are almost **instantaneous** .
- **Lower fees:** Fees for transactions on the Lightning Network are significantly lower than on the blockchain.
- **Scalability:** The Lightning Network allows Bitcoin to scale as transaction volumes grow.

Disadvantages:

- **Complexity:** The Lightning Network is technologically more complex than using the Bitcoin blockchain itself.
- **Security:** While the security of the underlying Bitcoins is guaranteed by the blockchain, there are additional risks with the Lightning Network, such as: B. the possibility that a channel node fails and the Bitcoins held in it are lost.
- **Adoption:** The Lightning Network is still in development and is not yet supported by all Bitcoin providers.

Conclusion:

The Lightning Network is a promising solution for Bitcoin scalability. It enables faster and cheaper transactions, which could increase the acceptance of Bitcoin in everyday life. However, there are also challenges that still need to be addressed in the future.

- *Use of the Lightning Network*

The Lightning Network (LN) offers a fast and affordable way to make Bitcoin payments. Here are the most important points for use:

Basics:

- **Offchain solution:** LN operates outside of the Bitcoin blockchain, making transactions faster and cheaper.

- **Payment channels:** Participants in the LN open bilateral channels in which they lock Bitcoins for transactions between themselves.
- **Routing:** Payments may go through multiple channels to get to the destination node.

Requirements:

- **Lightning Wallet:** You need a special wallet that supports LN. Popular options include Blue Wallet and Phoenix Wallet.
- **Bitcoin:** To use LN, you need Bitcoins, which you transfer to your LN wallet.

Process:

1. **Open a channel:** You and your trading partner open a channel with a set amount of Bitcoin.
2. **Transactions:** Within the channel, you can send as many payments back and forth as you want as long as the channel is open.
3. **Close channel:** As soon as you stop planning any further transactions, the channel will be closed and the remaining Bitcoins will be transferred back to the Bitcoin blockchain.

Advantages:

- **Fast transactions:** Payments on the LN network are almost instantaneous.
- **Low fees:** Transaction fees on LN are significantly lower than on the Bitcoin blockchain.
- **Privacy:** LN transactions are sometimes more anonymous than transactions on the blockchain.

Disadvantages:

- **Complexity:** Using LN requires technical understanding and involves certain risks.
- **New Technology:** LN is still in development and may be unstable.
- **Not all providers:** Not all Bitcoin providers support LN yet.

Where can I find more information?

To learn more about using the Lightning Network, you can use various sources:

- **Instructions on Lightning wallet provider websites:** These often provide detailed step-by-step instructions.
- **Online articles and tutorials:** There are numerous online resources that explain how LN works and how to use it.
- **Bitcoin communities:** Forums and discussion groups offer the opportunity to exchange ideas with other LN users and ask questions.

Chapter 9: Bitcoin and Blockchain Technology

- *Areas of application of blockchain*

Blockchain technology has the potential to revolutionize various industries and application areas. Here are some examples:

Finance:

- **Cryptocurrencies:** Bitcoin, Ethereum and other cryptocurrencies are based on blockchain technology.
- **Cross-border payments:** Blockchain can make transactions faster, cheaper and more transparent.
- **Securities trading:** Blockchain can make trading stocks, bonds and other assets more efficient and secure.

Supply chain:

- **Tracking of goods:** Blockchain can make the origin and transport of goods in the supply chain more transparent.
- **Counterfeit prevention:** Blockchain can ensure the authenticity of products and combat counterfeiting.
- **Supply Chain Optimization:** Blockchain can improve supply chain efficiency through smart contracts and automated processes.

Identity management:

- **Secure Identities:** Blockchain can store and manage people's identities securely and in a decentralized manner.
- **Self-determined data use:** Blockchain can give people control over their own data and allow them to decide who has access to it.
- **Identity theft prevention:** Blockchain can increase the security of identities and make identity theft more difficult.

Healthcare:

- **Electronic health records:** Blockchain can make the storage and exchange of health data more secure and efficient.
- **Medical Research:** Blockchain can improve researcher collaboration and use of health data for research.
- **Insurance:** Blockchain can make the processing of insurance claims more efficient and transparent.

Public administration:

- **Voting systems:** Blockchain can improve the security and transparency of elections.
- **Land Registration:** Blockchain can make the management of land titles and other assets more efficient and transparent.
- **Taxes:** Blockchain can make tax collection more efficient and fair.

These are just a few examples of the areas of application of blockchain technology. The potential of the technology is far from being exhausted and it is expected that further innovative applications will be developed in the coming years.

For more information, see:

- https://www.bundesnetzagentur.de/DE/Fachthemen/Digitalisierung/Technologien/Blockchain/BC_Netzsectors/start.html
- https://www.sap.com/products/artificial-intelligence/what-is-blockchain.html
- https://www.ibm.com/blockchain
- https://www.fit.fraunhofer.de/en/business-areas/cooperation-systems/blockchain.html
- https://ch.linkedin.com/in/julienweissenberg

- *Decentralized Applications (dApps)*

What are dApps ?

Decentralized applications (dApps) are software applications based on a decentralized network, such as a blockchain. Unlike traditional applications that run on a central server and are controlled by a single entity, dApps are :

- **Decentralized:** They run on a distributed network of computers, making them more resistant to failures and tampering.
- **Transparent:** The code of the dApps is visible to everyone, making the functionality of the application transparent and verifiable.

- **Secure:** The dApps' data is stored on the blockchain, which offers high security and immutability.
- **Permissionless :** dApps are accessible and usable by anyone without requiring permission from a central authority.

How do dApps work ?

dApps consist of two main components:

- **Smart Contracts :** These are self-governing programs that run on the blockchain. They set the rules and how the dApp works .
- **User Interface:** This is the graphical interface with which the dApp users interact.

Examples of dApps :

There are already a variety of dApps in different areas, such as: E.g.:

- **Decentralized Finance (DeFi):** dApps , which offer financial services such as lending, trading, and interest earning without requiring the involvement of banks or other financial institutions.
- **Games:** dApps , which allow players to own and trade digital assets, play games, and otherwise interact with other players.
- **Social networks:** dApps , which allow users to control their data and share their content in a decentralized manner.
- **Identity management:** dApps that allow users to self-manage and securely store their identities.

Advantages of dApps :

dApps offer several advantages over traditional applications, such as: E.g.:

- **Greater security:** dApps are better protected against hacker attacks and data manipulation thanks to blockchain technology.
- **More transparency:** The code and data of dApps are visible to everyone, making how the application works more transparent and auditable.
- **Less third-party control:** dApps are not controlled by a single entity, giving users more control over their data and their activities.
- **Greater freedom:** dApps are accessible and usable by anyone without requiring permission from a central authority.

Challenges of dApps :

dApps also face some challenges, such as: E.g.:

- **Complexity:** The development and use of dApps can be complex for non-technical users.
- **Scalability:** Most dApps are still in early stages of development and have not yet achieved the scalability to compete with traditional applications.
- **Regulation:** The legal framework for dApps is still unclear, which can lead to regulatory challenges.

Future of dApps :

dApps have the potential to fundamentally change the way we interact with software applications. The advantages of dApps , such as: Better security, more transparency and less third-party control could lead to dApps playing an increasingly important role in the future.

Additional Information:

- https://de.wikipedia.org/wiki/Dezentrales_Finanzwesen

- https://coinmarketcap.com/view/dapp/

- *The future of blockchain technology*

The future of blockchain technology is a topic of much speculation and debate. There are many different opinions about how technology will develop in the coming years and what impact it will have on different industries.

Potential of blockchain technology:

- **Decentralization and transparency:** Blockchain technology can help decentralize processes and make them more transparent. This can lead to greater trust and efficiency in various areas, such as: B. in finance, the supply chain and administration.
- **Security and data protection:** Blockchain technology offers a high level of security and data protection. The data in the blockchain is encrypted and immutable, which protects it from manipulation and hacker attacks.
- **Efficiency and automation:** Blockchain technology can make processes more efficient and automated. This can result in cost savings and faster processing of transactions.

Challenges of Blockchain Technology:

- **Scalability:** Blockchain technology in its current form is not yet scalable enough to be used for mass applications. However, solutions are being worked on to resolve this issue.
- **Regulation:** The regulation of blockchain technology is still unclear. There are still no uniform standards and laws regulating the use of the technology.
- **Acceptance:** The acceptance of blockchain technology is still relatively low. It is important to educate the public about the benefits of technology and instill confidence in how it works.

Possible areas of application:

- **Finance:** cryptocurrencies, decentralized financial systems (DeFi), payment processing
- **Supply chain:** tracking of goods, transparency in the supply chain, prevention of counterfeits
- **Administration:** identity management, digital voting, land registration
- **Healthcare:** data security, patient files, drug counterfeit protection
- **Energy industry:** decentralized energy markets, intelligent power grid

In conclusion, blockchain technology has great potential to revolutionize various industries. However, there are still some challenges that need to be overcome before the technology can reach its full potential.

Attachment

- **Glossary of important terms**

Bitcoin:

- A digital currency introduced by Satoshi Nakamoto in 2009.
- Decentralized and peer-to-peer, meaning there is no central authority controlling Bitcoin.
- Transactions are stored on a blockchain, a public and immutable ledger.

Blockchain:

- A decentralized database that stores transactions in blocks.
- Blocks are chained together, making the blockchain tamper-proof.
- The blockchain serves as the basis for Bitcoin and other cryptocurrencies.

Cryptocurrency:

- A digital currency that uses cryptography to secure transactions and generate new units.
- Bitcoin is the first and most well-known cryptocurrency, but there are many others.
- Cryptocurrencies can be used as a means of payment, investment or object of speculation.

Fiat currency:

- A currency issued by a government or central bank.

- Fiat currencies have no intrinsic value but are based on trust in the issuing institution.
- Examples of fiat currencies include euros, dollars and yen.

Satoshi:

- The smallest unit of Bitcoin.
- One Satoshi is one hundred millionth of a Bitcoin (0.00000001 BTC).
- Satoshis are often used for small transactions.

Mining:

- The process of validating transactions and adding new blocks to the blockchain.
- Miners use powerful computers to solve complex mathematical problems.
- As a reward for mining, miners receive new Bitcoins.

Wallet:

- A digital wallet that can be used to store Bitcoins.
- There are different types of wallets, e.g. E.g. software wallets, hardware wallets and paper wallets.
- Choosing the right wallet depends on the user's individual needs.

Halving :

- An event that occurs every four years in which the reward for mining Bitcoins is halved.
- The halving is intended to limit Bitcoin inflation.
- The last halving took place in May 2020.

Volatility:

- A measure of the price fluctuations of a cryptocurrency.
- Bitcoin is a very volatile cryptocurrency, meaning the price can fluctuate significantly.
- Investors should be aware of volatility before investing in Bitcoin.

Disclaimer:

- This information is for informational purposes only and does not constitute investment advice.
- Investing in cryptocurrencies is speculative and involves a high degree of risk.
- Investors should only invest money that they can afford to lose.

Additional resources:

- Bitcoin Wiki: https://en.bitcoin.it/wiki/Main_Page
- Bitcoin Core: https://bitcoincore.org/
- Block Explorer : https://www.blockchain.com/explorer

A notice:

- This glossary is not exhaustive and there are many other terms relevant to Bitcoin.
- It is important to educate yourself and understand the risks before investing in Bitcoin.

- *Resources for further information*

Sites:

- **Bitcoin Core:** https://bitcoin.org/en/bitcoin-core/ - The official website of the Bitcoin Core software, with information about how Bitcoin works, downloads, and more.
- **Bitcoin Wiki:** https://en.wikipedia.org/wiki/Bitcoin - A comprehensive wiki with information on all aspects of Bitcoin, from history and technology to wallets and exchanges.
- **Blockstream :** https://blockstream.com/ - A company specializing in the development of Bitcoin technology, with a variety of resources including blog posts, webinars and research papers.
- **CoinDesk :** https://www.coindesk.com/ - A news platform specializing in Bitcoin and cryptocurrencies in general, with breaking news, analysis and prices.

Books:

- **The Bitcoin standard:** https://saifedean.com/tbs - By Andreas M. Antonopoulos - A book that explains the basics of Bitcoin and why it is important.
- **The Internet of Money:** https://www.amazon.com/Internet-Money-Andreas-M-Antonopoulos/dp/1537000454 - By Andreas M. Antonopoulos - A book that examines the potential impact of Bitcoin on the global economy.

- **Mastering Bitcoin:** https://github.com/bitcoinbook/bitcoinbook - By Andreas M. Antonopoulos - A technical guide that explains how Bitcoin works in detail.

Videos:

- **Bitcoin: The Future of Money?** https://www.reuters.com/business/future-of-money/ - A documentary exploring the history and potential of Bitcoin.
- **What is Bitcoin?** https://www.investopedia.com/terms/b/bitcoin.asp - A short explainer video from Khan Academy.
- **How Bitcoin Works** https://www.investopedia.com/news/how-bitcoin-works/ - An explanatory video by Andreas M. Antonopoulos .

Subreddits:

- **r/Bitcoin:** https://www.reddit.com/r/Bitcoin/ - The largest Bitcoin community on Reddit.
- **r/ BitcoinBeginners** : https://www.reddit.com/r/BitcoinBeginners/ - A subreddit for Bitcoin newbies.
- **r/ BitcoinMarkets** : https://www.reddit.com/r/BitcoinMarkets/ - A subreddit for discussions about the Bitcoin market.

Forums:

- **Bitcointalk :** https://bitcointalk.org/ - The largest Bitcoin forum in the world.

- **Stack Exchange:** https://bitcoin.stackexchange.com/ - A Q&A platform for Bitcoin developers and users.

Note: This is just a small selection of resources. There are many other websites, books, videos and forums that contain information about Bitcoin.

More tips:

- **Start with the basics:** Make sure you understand the basics of Bitcoin before moving on to more advanced topics.
- **Be critical:** There are many different opinions about Bitcoin. Be critical of the information you read and form your own opinion.
- **Be careful:** Bitcoin is a new technology and there are risks associated with it. Be careful when trading or investing in Bitcoin.

- **List of Bitcoin exchanges and wallets**

Bitcoin exchanges are platforms where you can buy and sell Bitcoins. They act as intermediaries between buyers and sellers and typically offer a range of features such as: B. the ability to use different payment methods, place different order types and track prices.

Here are some popular Bitcoin exchanges:

- **Coinbase:** One of the largest and most popular exchanges in the world, offering a user-friendly interface and a wide range of features.

 ɔinbase

[Opens in a new window](https://1000logos.net)
1000logos.net

Coinbase logo

- **Kraken:** Another large exchange with a good reputation for security and reliability.

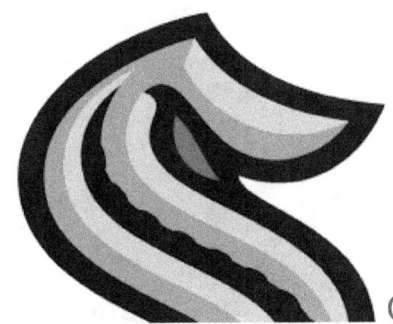

[Opens in a new window](https://en.wikipedia.org)
en.wikipedia.org

Octopus logo

- **Bitpanda :** A European exchange that offers a wide range of cryptocurrencies and fiat currencies for trading.

bitpan

[Opens in a new window](#)
B www.bitpanda.com

Bitpanda logo

- **Bison:** A German exchange operated by the Stuttgart Stock Exchange and aimed at beginners.

[Opens in a new window](#)
S scalebranding.com

Bison logo

- **bitcoin.de:** A German exchange that has existed since 2011 and is a good option for experienced traders.

itcoin-Marktplatz Opens in a new window

www.bitcoin.de

bitcoin.de logo

Bitcoin wallets:

Bitcoin wallets are digital wallets where you can safely store your Bitcoins. There are different types of wallets, e.g. B. Hardware wallets, software wallets and online wallets.

Hardware wallets:

Hardware wallets are physical devices that store your Bitcoins offline. They are considered the safest way to store Bitcoins because they cannot be hacked even if your computer is infected.

Some popular hardware wallets are:

- **Ledger Nano S:** A popular hardware wallet that is easy to use and supports a wide range of cryptocurrencies.

[Opens in a new window](#)
shop.ledger.com

Ledger Nano S logo

- **Trezor Model One :** Another popular hardware wallet that is compatible with a wide range of cryptocurrencies.

[Opens in a new window](#)
www.coinbureau.com

Trezor Model One logo

Software wallets:

Software wallets are digital wallets that are installed on your computer or smartphone. While they are not as secure as hardware wallets, they are still a good option for storing smaller amounts of Bitcoin.

Some popular software wallets are:

- **Electrum:** A free and open source software wallet known for its security and ease of use.

Opens in a new window ⓢ seeklogo.com

Electrum logo

- **Exodus:** An easy-to-use software wallet that offers a wide range of features such as: B. the ability to store multiple cryptocurrencies.

Opens in a new window
www.deviantart.com

Exodus logo

Online wallets:

Online wallets are web-based wallets offered by exchanges or other providers. While they are convenient to use, they are also considered the most insecure way to store Bitcoins as they are vulnerable to hacks.

It is therefore recommended to store your Bitcoins in a hardware wallet or a software wallet that you control yourself.

Important NOTE:

This list is not exhaustive and is for informational purposes only. Before using a Bitcoin exchange or wallet, you should do your own research and make sure they are reputable and safe.